How Indian Emily Saved Fort Davis

Larry Francell

Purple Feather Press · Texas

Copyright © 2021 by Lawrence J. Francell All rights reserved.

This work was originally published in The Journal of Big Bend Studies, Volume 29, published by the Center for Big Bend Studies at Sul Ross State University, 2017 under the title "How Indian Emily Saved Fort Davis: A Legend Revisited."

Cover Illustration: The well-travelled post card of Indian Emily's "grave" by Big Bend photographer Peter Koch. (Author's collection)

This book or any portion thereof may not be reproduced or used in any manner whatsoever without the express written permission of the publisher except for the use of brief quotations in a book review.

Printed in the United States of America

Third Printing, December 2021
Second Printing, October 2021
First Printing, June 2021

ISBN 978-1-7353805-2-0

Purple Feather Press
513 Debora Dr
Georgetown, TX 78628

www.PurpleFeatherPress.com

How Indian Emily Saved
Fort Davis

How Indian Emily Saved Fort Davis

From the day the National Park Service took possession of Fort Davis as a National Historic Site, the legend of Indian Emily proved a thorn in the side of the staff developing an interpretive plan for the post. This was especially true during the early days of the historic site when this folk tale was still fresh in the mind of the general public. It was particularly a problem for Frank Smith, superintendent in the late 1960's through early 1970's[1]. Frank was described by the folklorist at Sul Ross, Elton Miles, when asked about the story, "he snorted and scoffed at the Indian Emily tale and told me it must have been lifted right out of a Harold Bell Wright novel."[2] Wright was a

---

[1] I worked for Frank Smith as a Seasonal Ranger during the summers 1967 and 1968. We became friends and he was great mentor. By then Indian Emily controversy had mostly gone away but it was still a sore point with Frank.
[2] Dr. Elton Miles, *Tales of the Big Bend*, (College Station: Texas A&M Press, 1976), p. 103.

bestselling romantic writer in the first half of the 20th Century and probably best known for *The Shepard of the Hills*.[3]

Frank had much to do with the early interpretive plans for the fort, including coordinating with the Army at Fort Sill to create the Retreat Parade sound program, and began the push for the interior restoration of the several building we can visit today. He was merciless in the quest for the best possible interpretation of Fort Davis to the general public, backed up this interpretation with quality research, and demanded the best from his employees. Thus the mere mention of Indian Emily would send him into apoplexy. If anyone could be accused of killing Indian Emily, it was Frank Smith.

So what's all the fuss about? There are several minor variations that we shall explore, but in essence the story goes that the Apaches raided Fort Davis but

---

[3] *The Shepard of the Hills* (1907) is still in print, including an electronic copy available on Amazon. A movie version (1941) starring John Wayne is available on DVD.

How Indian Emily Saved Fort Davis

were beaten back by the soldiers and possibly some civilians, and in the aftermath a young Indian woman was left behind, or possibly wounded and captured in the ensuing pursuit. Of indeterminate age, but described as young, the girl was taken in by the mother of Lieutenant Thomas Easton with whom she lived for months, or years, also an indeterminate period. Mrs. Easton named her Emily. Emily eventually fell in love with young Lt. Easton, but Easton was in love with Mary Nelson, possibly the sister of another young lieutenant. When the impending marriage was announced, Emily, becoming despondent ran away back to her own people.

At some point in time after she returned, Emily learned that the Apaches were once again going to attack the garrison at Fort Davis, and her loyalty to Mrs. Easton and love for Thomas prompted her to return to the fort and raise the alarm. As she tried to return, she was challenged by a sentry with the standard, "halt, who goes there." Not answering she was shot and wounded by the sentry, who evidently recognized her as the Indian girl known as Emily and had her taken to the Easton quarters. Once there, and before she died, Emily was able to warn the garrison of the impending attack, which was beaten off with alacrity. Thus the tale of Indian Emily.

Earl Francell, the author's father, inspects a sign posted at a Fort Davis Officer's Quarters (c.1950). While at any time the post garrison might contain a "few hundred soldiers," a "thousand Apache warriors" would represent an historically impossible number. (Author's collection)

How Indian Emily Saved Fort Davis

While there may be other written accounts of the story, only four count. Any others were taken from these, all of which had close contact with Fort Davis. According to Elton Miles, and my research, the first published account is in Carlysle Graham Rath's *Romance of the Davis Mountains,* printed in 1919 and republished in 1963. Rath's very first sentence in the Preface of the 1963 publication states, "I claim no literary merit for this work." No truer words were probably ever written, but Rath can be forgiven somewhat as the first person to actually delve into the history of the region.[4]

One of Rath's traveling companions and research assistants was Barry Scobee who settled in Fort Davis

---

[4] Carlysle Graham Rath, *The Romance of the Davis Mountains and Big Bend Country,* (Odessa, Texas: The Rathbooks Company, 1963). I have searched for the 1919 first edition of Rath, but have never found one available, but surely one exists.

and became the local historian, one of the organizers of the local historical society, and an early promoter of Fort Davis as either a state or national park. However, Scobee was first and foremost a newspaperman who worked as a stringer for area papers including San Angelo and Fort Worth.

In 1936, at the suggestion of J. Frank Dobie, he published a pamphlet on the history of Fort Davis as part of the WPA Writers' Project.[5] In 1965 members of the Historical Society, at the instigation of some of the community, renamed the mountain north of town for Scobee. This in itself was a problem since the mountain was at the time named, albeit informally, after Trinidad Granado, an early settler and family patriarch. This situation was corrected during the Fourth of July celebration in 2016 with the dedication of a second marker.

---

[5] Lucy Miller Jacobson, *Jeff Davis County, Texas*, (Fort Davis: Fort Davis Historical Society, 1993), pp. 586-587.

How Indian Emily Saved Fort Davis

Over time Scobee wrote this pamphlet and two other books on the history of Fort Davis. The pamphlet, titled *The Story of Fort Davis*, was published by Marvin Hunter, Publisher and Editor of the *Dispatch*, the local newspaper then and now.[6] Scobee's second effort was titled *Old Fort Davis* and was published by the Naylor Company in San Antonio in 1947. I have five copies of this book and no two are alike. One has a beige cover, one a marbled brown cover, one a solid brown cover with dust jacket, one a blue cover with dust jacket, and one with a light brown marbled cover. I have owned two others with the dark brown marbled cover, which I have given to friends. Interestingly the blue copy is dimensionally smaller than all the others. This seems to be the least common copy. However, all

---

[6] Barry Scobee, *The Story of Fort Davis: Jeff Davis County and the Davis Mountains*, (Fort Davis: Marvin Hunter, Jr., 1936). While I knew of the existence of this publication, I never saw one until I visited an estate book sale for a family relative. Opening the cover I discovered the inscription: *To C. Espy Miller with regrets, apologies, and regards! Barry Scobee, Fort Davis, June 18, 1936.* Espy Miller was my wife's grandfather, and I was pleased to "recover" this book before it was sold.

five have the same publisher, publication date and the same text.[7]

Finally Scobee published his *opus maximus* in 1963 titled *Fort Davis Texas* with no comma for some reason. As an accomplished newspaperman he certainly knew good grammar. Published by Hill Printing Company of El Paso, the author sought to bring a greater degree of historical accuracy to this effort.[8]

As stated, according to Elton Miles, Rath was the first to publish the Indian Emily story. As a folklorist, Miles places the tale in the genre of folklore known as the "lover's leap" story wherein there is an unrequited love and a lover who sacrifices herself, usually a woman. (Men never seem to leap from cliffs due to unrequited love.) Miles also states that this "motif has

---

[7] Barry Scobee, *Old Fort Davis*, (San Antonio: The Naylor Company, 1947). Regardless of the issue of bindings, every complete copy should have five double page photo paper illustrations and two single page photo illustrations. Many of the copies found in in bookstores have been cut.

[8] Barry Scobee, *Fort Davis Texas, 1583-1960*, (El Paso: Hill Printing Company 1963).

attached itself to several old army posts throughout the United States."[9] My research has not discovered any of these other army posts, but nor has my research been comprehensive. Frankly, I think it a story that is purely Fort Davis. Miles also states that Rath claimed that he heard the story from none other than Henry Flipper in El Paso. Flipper, the first African-American to graduate from West Point, served at Fort Davis and was court-marshaled there on charges of embezzlement and conduct unbecoming an officer. Found not guilty of the first charge he was nonetheless found guilty of the second and dismissed from service.[10] Trained at West Point, he went on to make a name for himself as an engineer and surveyor. It is interesting that Flipper would pass on a tale such as this having served at Fort Davis during the primary period of conflict with the Apaches.

---

[9] Miles, p. 100.
[10] Charles Robinson, III, *The Court Martial of Henry Flipper*, (El Paso: The University of Texas at El Paso 1994), p. 111. Flipper was not cashiered, but merely dismissed, the Army basically saying they no longer needed his services.

Regardless of origin, Rath accepted the story whole cloth from somewhere. Details vary between Rath and Scobee, but the gist of the story remains the same. In the original version published by Rath the Apache attack was made on the town with no mention of the garrison at the Fort. The Indians were beaten off by "soldiers and citizens" who were "aided by the presence of several large freight outfits, which had camped in Fort Davis on their way over the Chihuahua Trail."[11] In Scobee's 1936 version the Apaches attacked the Fort when most of the soldiers were away, but the attack was once again repulsed with the aid of the freight outfits camped nearby.

In Scobee's 1947 version he virtually plagiarizes Rath, quoting almost verbatim with the attack occurring on the town. In Scobee's 1963 book, he merely provides a synopsis of the story, stating "a young Apache girl was captured in a fight with Indians and brought to the Fort."[12] This is a means for Scobee

---

[11] Rath, p. 170.
[12] Scobee, *Fort Davis Texas*, p. 56.

How Indian Emily Saved Fort Davis

to keep the story alive in the face of the research being done by the National Park Service Historian Robert Utley.

All of the versions are consistent when it comes to what happened after the Apache girl was brought to the fort to live. She was taken in by a Mrs. Easton who named her Emily. Easton had a son Thomas who was a lieutenant. Emily was old enough to be taken with Tom, but Tom fell in love with another young woman at the Fort, Mary Nelson. None of the versions explain if Mary Nelson was the daughter of another officer or the daughter of a civilian. Her parents are never named, nor is Tom's father. However, it is Barry Scobee who gives Mary a first name, which Rath does not.

The Jeff Davis County history book written by Lucy Jacobson, while not definitive, but rather comprehensive, does not list any Nelson's as civilians in Fort Davis in the period, and to her credit when she wrote this book, Jacobson steered completely away from the Indian Emily story. According to Elton Miles, a Sul Ross State University graduate student, Bruce Lamberson, found passing evidence of a Mr. Nelson in Fort Davis.[13] A civilian named Nelson may be inconclusive, but not so in the case of an Army officer.

It is here that the research becomes interesting. One of the most valuable reference books, and one that I always keep close at hand, is Francis Heitman's *Historical Register and Dictionary of the United States Army from its Organization, September 29, 1789 to March 2, 1903*.[14] Heitman lists every officer, including officers who resigned from Federal service and joined the Confederacy, who served in the Army during the late 18th Century and the 19th Century.

In that period there were two Easton's who served, none named Thomas. There was Alpha Templeton Easton, a captain in the 14th Volunteer Infantry during the Spanish-American War and Langdon Cheves

---

[13] Miles, p. 104.
[14] Francis Heitman, *Historical Register and Dictionary of the United States Army from its Organization September 29, 1789 to March 2, 1903,* 2 volume reprint, (Urbana: University of Illinois, 1965).

How Indian Emily Saved Fort Davis

Easton who graduated twenty-second in his West Point Class of 1833, and spent his entire career in the Quartermaster Corps rising to the rank of major general by the end of the Civil War and cited for "distinguished and important service" in the Atlanta, Georgia Campaign. He died in 1884, never serving in the Southwest.

Considering that Mary Nelson might have been the daughter of an officer serving at Fort Davis, as implied by Scobee, Heitman lists nineteen Nelson's who served during the period. Eight served in the Pre-Civil War Army, three served in the Spanish-American War only, and the balance served in the Civil War. None ever saw duty west of the Mississippi. So the question is, how did these specific names come to be attached to the Indian Emily story? For that I have no answer.

The Indian Emily story culminates with her return to her people, her discovery of another attack to be perpetrated on the garrison, her attempt to warn the fort, and ensuing wounding by a sentry as she tries to sneak back to the Easton house. She dies in the presence of Mrs. Easton according to Rath gasping, "All my people come to kill. I hear talk. By light of morning. Maybe you know. Tom no get killed. Goodbye."[15] Words Scobee repeats verbatim in his 1947 book only. Once again contemporary research and sources are helpful in understanding that this story is legend, not fact.

"The Death of Indian Emily"
Oil on board, No Date, Artist Unknown
The artist had some passing knowledge of Fort Davis. The background mountains work and architectural elements of existing buildings are present, but there is no structure that matches the painting.
(Gift of John Avant)

---

[15] Rath, p. 171.

How Indian Emily Saved Fort Davis

※

By 1963 Scobee was partially ready to admit defeat. While he repeats the gist of the story, he does state the "evidence to support the Indian Emily story is scanty."[16] His suggestion for the factual basis is a fight that took place in the Horse Head Hills (the Santiago mountain range north of Big Bend National Park) on September 8, 1868. Lt. Patrick Cusack with elements of the 9th Cavalry attacked an Apache camp. Upon his return to Fort Davis he had two rescued Mexican boys and a captured infant Apache girl.[17]

For this action Cusack would receive the brevet rank of captain, but nothing appears in the record relative to the infant. Likely she was given over to a civilian family. Had she been adopted by an Army family there would have been a more complete record. Even Scobee,

---

[16] Scobee, *Fort Davis Texas*, p. 57.
[17] Robert Utley, *Special Report on Fort Davis, Texas*, (Santa Fe: National Park Service, 1960), p. 65.

after suggesting this child may have been the genesis of the Indian Emily story, makes no further mention.

The Apaches that were engaged with the U.S. Army in this period were guerilla fighters using hit and run tactics, avoiding set piece engagements where they were outnumbered. Fort Davis was never attacked by Indians.[18] The forts had nothing to offer other than well-trained and well-armed soldiers. It was far easier to attack isolated homesteads, stagecoaches and small groups of travelers on the road than to take on a major garrison at an established fort. According to the Indian Emily legend, Fort Davis was attacked not once, but twice, and (according to all records) this just did not happen.

So based upon all this evidence, is there anything in the record that might support the legend? There was, in fact, an Indian woman who was captured and lived

---

[18] Peter Cozzens, *The Earth is Weeping: The Epic Story of the Indian Wars for the American West*, (New York: Alfred A. Knopf, 2016), p. 377. On September 1, 1881 a small band of Apaches briefly attacked Fort Apache, Arizona making this the only time any of the Southwestern forts were directly attacked.

How Indian Emily Saved Fort Davis

at the fort for a period of time. On January 29, 1881, the Texas Ranger's under the command of Capt. George Baylor and Lt. C.L. Nevill attacked a remnant of Chief Victorio's band high in the Sierra Diablo. In the firefight a woman and two children were captured. Nevill, stationed in the community of Fort Davis at the time, took the captives to the post where the children were adopted by the Hospital Steward and his wife. The family name was Wesseck and the children stayed with the family well after he left the Army.[19]

The woman lived at the post and according to Robert Utley's research, the Post Surgeon's Report of January 1882, stated, "A cowardly and brutal murder of an Indian captive was perpetrated by some party or parties unknown near the Hospital where the woman was tented. The deed was done with an axe or some other sharp instrument - her head being split open, and rape seems to be the object."[20] This woman was

---

[19] Utley, p. 89.
[20] Ibid.

neither young enough to be Emily, nor was she taken in by a post family, especially one named Easton.

Regardless the story lived on. In January 1940 an article by Buren Sparks titled "Emily the Indian Squaw" was published in *Frontier Times* magazine. It repeats the Rath/Scobee story with some embellishment. After Emily ran away, "The alarm was given and soldiers and citizens rode forth in search of the disconsolate maid. For days the search went on in canyons, caves, and the valley to the south, but still no Emily."[21] With present research, this part of the story appears nowhere else.

Virginia Madison in her book *The Big Bend Country of Texas* published in 1955 repeats the Rath and early Scobee versions, with the additional statement that Emily ran off on the very day of the announced engagement between Tom and Mary.[22] Also sometime

---

[21] Boren Sparks, "Emily, the Indian Squaw," Frontier Times. Vol.17, No. 4, (January 1940).
[22] Virginia Madison, *The Big Bend Country of Texas* (Albuquerque: University of New Mexico Press, 1955), pp. 38-39.

How Indian Emily Saved Fort Davis

in this period, the story again went national with publication in *The West* magazine.[23]

The most interesting take on the story was in a book of poems published in 1948 by Faye Carr Adams. In the poem titled "Em'ly the Chieftain's Daughter," Adams promoted Emily to an Indian princess and added drama to the story through her turgid verse:

> The sentry called and who should come
> But the captain she loved so dear,
> He lifted her and called her name -----
> And then death held no fear.[24]

Tom Easton even received a promotion from lieutenant to captain out of the deal. In 1970 and 1971 Faye Carr Adams was the official alternate Poet Laurate of Texas (always the bridesmaid, never the bride). Her several books of poetry are still available on Amazon, so there is no way to tell how far her Indian Emily poem was dispersed.

---

[23] Miles, p. 175.
[24] Ibid., p. 105.

Larry Francell

In 1936, Texas celebrated its Centennial. The Legislature created the Commission of Control for the Texas Centennial in 1935, allocating $3,000,000 for the effort, an amount matched by Congress. As part of the celebration numerous markers, statues and buildings were dedicated. The Museum of the Big Bend at Sul Ross State University was one of the buildings created for the Centennial. Historic markers were placed throughout the state.[25] Most of the markers were cut from gray granite and one of those was placed at the old cemetery at Fort Davis memorializing Indian Emily. When the post was abandoned all remains of military personnel were moved to the National Cemetery in San Antonio, so even Barry Scobee admits the location of the marker was a guess.

Not publicized at the time, nor even now, but in 1967 when I was working as a seasonal ranger at the fort, there was an archeological survey conducted by

---

[25] Dr. Ron Tyler, ed., *Handbook of Texas*, "Texas Centennial." Vol. 6, (Austin: Texas State Historical Association, 1996), pp. 297-298.

How Indian Emily Saved Fort Davis

Park Service personnel to uncover the foundation remains of the first, 1854 post. Frank Smith had them open what was purported to be the grave next to the centennial marker, but no human remains were present.

Texas Centennial Marker at Indian Emily's "grave" in what was the Fort Davis Post Cemetery. Because the Fort Davis property was leased, not owned, by the Federal Government, soldiers were disinterred and moved to the National Cemetery at Fort Sam Houston, San Antonio. (Author's collection)

Early in this century, before Jerry Yarbrough retired from the Park Service, he had the marker removed and placed in storage. In the meantime countless numbers visited Indian Emily's "grave" especially in the period between 1936 and the mid-60s.

However, the greatest national dissemination of the Indian Emily story came on November 26, 1959 when the television show *Death Valley Days* presented an episode titled, "Indian Emily." I actually remember seeing this episode at age 14 in Odessa. For any interested party this was Season Eight, Episode Seven. It was a fair representation of the Indian Emily story, compiled from both Rath and Scobee, and romantically expanded to a 30 minute format.[26]

Indian Emily is played by Jolene Brand with a career mostly in episodic television. Poor Lieutenant

---

[26] *Google* Search. *Death Valley Days.*

How Indian Emily Saved Fort Davis

Tom Easton, mostly oblivious to what is going on around him, is played by Burt Metcalfe, who also worked in television series, but came to recognition as a writer and then producer on the series *M*A*S*H*. Mrs. Easton (there is no Mr. Easton) is played by Meg Wyllie with a long career in television including the villain in the first episode of *Star Trek*.

In the Indian Emily legend there is no "bad guy," but in a television series there must be at least a degree of good versus evil. In this instance the Army Scout holds that position. Scragg, with no last name but a name that says it all, is played by Bing Russell, another television regular and father of the more famous actor, Kurt Russell. In the show, he is the one who captured Emily, and warns everyone not to trust "an Apache on the loose." He is also the one who shoots her as she returns to warn the garrison. The sentry says to Scragg, "did you hear anything?" To which Scragg replies, "Yeah, it's an Indian." He then shoots Emily. Only as she lays dying does he see the light and apologizes. A little late, I thought.

Larry Francell

A cursory search for the episode's director, Edward Ludlum, and writer, John Alexander, uncovered nothing useful. However, there are enough references to the original legend that someone must have had access to the Carl Rath/ Barry Scobee versions. Although the "fort" is surrounded by a stockade and looks like the sets used often by John Ford and numerous other television series, it is consistently referred to as Fort Davis, and Emily is captured by a patrol on a scout through Limpia Canyon, not a common name at all.

The episode ends, as do all the *Death Valley Days*, with Stanley Andrews, The Old Ranger, bringing closure. According to The Old Ranger, Emily was buried with full military honors, "but the Emily's story did not end in that shallow grave. The drama of great romance and sacrifice so endeared her to the State of Texas that they have erected a monument in her memory at Fort Davis in Jefferson (sic) Davis County."

How Indian Emily Saved Fort Davis

At the time *Death Valley Days* was one of the most successful syndicated TV shows, sponsored by 20 Mule Team Borax, a mineral mined in Death Valley. The introduction included a shot of a 20 mule team pulling tandem wagons across the desolation of Death Valley. Originated in 1930 the program ran on radio until 1945. Resurrected for television in 1952 it ran until 1970. It's most famous host, and sometimes star, was Ronald Reagan, but the original host Stanley Andrews was the host from 1952 until 1963, the period during which the "Emily" episode aired.

Thus the Indian Emily story had a degree of national exposure, and certainly plenty of local exposure, especially by Scobee and the other members of the Fort Davis Historical Society who spent years promoting the old post as either a state park or national historic site.

The Fort Davis Historical Society was organized in February 1953 in the home of Malcolm "Bish" Tweedy, who lived on Officer's Row and was the concessionaire at the old post. Tweedy, along with a number of community leaders, was greatly concerned about the condition of the old fort and its continuing deterioration. In subsequent meetings a mission for the Society was written and, in part, a stated goal was, "the acquisition and preservation of the old Fort Davis Army Post and the acquisition, preservation and marking of historical landmarks in the Davis Mountains area." This mission also included the creation of a museum, which was accomplished within the Trading Post structure, a block building used as the concession and built on the foundation of one of the old barracks. That structure, non-historic, has long since been removed.[27]

This was a large task for a small community, but the Society set out to accomplish this mission. The most prominent and important achievement was the highly successful Fort Centennial Celebration in October 1954. The Odessa Chuckwagon Gang was invited to serve barbecue, which was how I came to be at this celebration, as my father was a member of the Gang.

---

[27] Jacobson, pp. 337-346.

How Indian Emily Saved Fort Davis

There was a parade that started at the hospital and went around the Parade Ground, a rodeo, and in the evenings a dance. But the center piece of the festival was the Indian Emily Pageant. Directed by Herbert Smith, the Superintendent of Schools, the pageant starred Roxa Medley as Emily.[28]

Fort Davis 1954 Centennial. State Senator H.L. Winfield, John G. Prude, Roxa Medley (Indian Emily), Barry Scobee, U.S. Representative J.T. Rutherford (L-R) (Fort Davis Historical Society Collection)

In attendance at the Centennial was J.T. Rutherford, at the time State Senator, but soon to be

---

[28] Ibid., p. 339.

the Congressman for West Texas. Rutherford grew up in Odessa but joined the Marines before he could graduate. He landed on Tarawa, Saipan, Tinian, and came home a local hero. Eventually he was awarded his high school diploma and graduated from Sul Ross State University and Baylor Law. A life-long Democrat he served four terms in Congress. J.T. was one of the few Texans to vote for the Civil Rights Bill, was one of the first Texans to come out in support of John Kennedy for president, and was a life-long friend of Lyndon Johnson.[29]

---

[29] Personal Research File on J.T. Rutherford. On November 3, 2012 former Congressman J.T. Rutherford was honored by Sul Ross State University as a Distinguished Alumni, where I was asked to provide an introduction. I once met Congressman Rutherford, who had gone to high school with my mother and was a friend of my father's. The information about Rutherford comes from Martha Francell's Odessa High School Annual, and information supplied by Ann Rutherford, his daughter, which includes a copy of an Obituary from The Odessa *American* (November, 10, 2006) written by Larry L. King, writer and a former aide to Rutherford. Mr. Rutherford died November 6, 2006. When I worked at Fort Davis National Historic Site (1967) I toured Mr. King around the site and he told me that he had written the legislation to create the National Historic Site.

How Indian Emily Saved Fort Davis

Rutherford was the first chairman of the House Subcommittee on National Parks. A strong supporter of Fort Davis he soon found himself in a position to make a significant move, one that would protect Fort Davis in perpetuity. The word was that President Kennedy wanted Cape Cod declared a National Seashore, but did not have the support to make it happen. Rutherford also knew that the California delegation to Congress wanted Point Reyes declared a National Seashore, but did not have enough support. He wanted Fort Davis saved as a National Historic Site and was able to broker a deal. President Kennedy got what he wanted, the California delegation what it wanted, and J.T. Rutherford tucked little Fort Davis into the deal. Believing the Indian Emily story to be true he used the legend in Congress to bolster his case with his fellow Congressmen, as did Ralph Yarbrough in the Senate.[30]

---

[30] Email from Ann Rutherford, October 30, 2012 and Larry King obituary. (Personal Research File on J.T. Rutherford).

Larry Francell

Rutherford and Senator Yarbrough introduced bills in Congress to accept Fort Davis into the NPS system (House Resolution 10352). The bills passed in September 1961, and in March 1962 Rutherford pushed through an appropriations bill for $449,300 for the actual purchase of the property, 447 acres. Fort Davis National Historic Site was officially created on July 4, 1963 and dedicated April 4, 1966.[31]

⚲

The story does not end here. With Frank Smith and Robert Utley on one side and Barry Scobee and numerous amateur historians and regional politicians on the other, the controversy over Emily lived on, culminating in the removal of the State Centennial

---

[31] Michael Walsh, *A Special Place, A Sacred Trust: Preserving the Fort Davis Story,* The Administrative History of Fort Davis National Historic Site, (Santa Fe: National Park Service, 1996), p. 82.

Marker by Jerry Yarbrough. One of the major issues in this controversy came when Superintendent Smith and the National Park Service interpretative staff, desiring to return the Fort to its original configuration, ceased access by automobile. Before the Park Service one could drive around the parade ground and out to the Indian Emily grave marker. Because the distance to walk was so great, it was blocking this access that generated some of the greatest controversy.

On the surface Barry Scobee continued to support the interpretative efforts of Park Service Historian Robert Utley, who he called "the Kid." However, Indian Emily remained an issue for him.[32] Shortly after the dedication in 1966, Scobee chose to correspond with State Senator Dorsey Hardeman of San Angelo about how his pet story had been mistreated by Smith. Hardeman, a politician and not a historian, was especially incensed that vehicular traffic to the grave marker had been denied. Complaining to U.S. Senator Ralph Yarbrough, he wrote, "The story of Indian Emily

---

[32] Jacobson, p. 341.

is so firmly established as a part of the heritage of this state, and particularly of the Davis Mountains area, that to preclude convenient public access to her grave would be to destroy a beautiful legend of our heritage."[33] Yarbrough replied, "I agree with you thoroughly about the treatment of Indian Emily's grave. Prior to receipt of your letter at the end of last week, I did not know her grave and the tradition were being treated as they are by the Park Service. I will begin work immediately to try to have this slight to one of our state's heroines, one of the great traditions of the West, one of the legends of Fort Davis, corrected."[34]

Frank Smith, recognizing the important role Scobee had played in creating the historic site, took the long view and, rather than argue the point, determined to continue to overwhelm the legend with quality research and the most accurate interpretative plan

---

[33] Welsh, p. 155.
[34] U. S. Senator Ralph Yarbrough to State Senator Dorsey Hardeman, August 22, 1966. (Personal Research File on J.T. Rutherford).

How Indian Emily Saved Fort Davis

possible. In his response to Senator Yarbrough, Frank stated that the road closed to the site was part of the Park Service attempt to "eliminate automobiles, roads, and parking areas that in our judgment would seriously mar the historic appearance and character that the restoration program is intended to create."[35] It is this ability for the visitor to step onto the post grounds and step back in history without the trappings of the modern world that makes Fort Davis a unique experience today.

Regardless of the ensuing controversy, the legend of Indian Emily had a profound effect on the creation of Fort Davis National Historic Site. While the story turns out to be pure legend, it is impossible to discount

---

[35] Welsh, p. 157. As Welsh writes, "Superintendent Smith's concern about the impact of the Indian Emily story on his park was not merely governmental pettiness, despite the claims of local and national politicians. He was determined to tell the Fort Davis tale as accurately as possible because of his long connection to the museum profession; a link that he cultivated assiduously during his six year tenure as the historic site." It was Frank's friendship and absolute dedication to historic interpretation that set me on a career course of forty years in the museum profession. When Frank died Jerry Yarbrough, then superintendent at the Fort, allowed his ashes to be scattered on the Parade Ground at the site he loved.

the value of this tale to the creation of the National Historic Site. While Fort Davis was, and is, the most intact of all the Southwestern garrisons from the Indian Wars, it is still one of many. Without the romantic story of Emily and her love for Tom Easton that was disseminated far and wide by Carl Rath, Barry Scobee, various other writers, Fort Davis would not stand out as someplace special. Without national exposure through venues such as *Death Valley Days*, the dedication of the Fort Davis Historical Society, and the support J.T. Rutherford, the country might still have a National Historic Site, but the path would have been much more difficult and time consuming.

How Indian Emily Saved Fort Davis

For many years after the National Historic Site opened, Indian Emily's story was part of the community. (Collection of Jennifer & Richard Harrod)

Larry Francell

Bibliography

Cozzens, Peter. *The Earth is Weeping: The Epic Story of the Indian Wars for the American West.* New York: Alfred A. Knopf, 2016.

Francell, Larry. Personal Research File on J.T. Rutherford.

Heitman, Francis. *Historic Register and Dictionary of the United States Army 1789-1903.* Urbana: University of Illinois Press, 1956.

Jacobson, Lucy. *Jeff Davis County, Texas.* Fort Davis: Fort Davis Historical Society, 1996.

Madison, Virginia. *The Big Bend Country of Texas.* Albuquerque: University of New Mexico Press, 1955.

Miles, Dr. Elton. *Tales of the Big Bend.* College Station: Texas A&M Press, 1976.

Rath, Carlysle Graham. *The Romance of the Davis Mountains and Big Bend Country.* Odessa, Texas: Rathbooks, 1963.

Robinson, Charles III. *The Court Martial of Henry Flipper.* El Paso: The University of Texas at El Paso Press, 1994.

Scobee, Barry. *Fort Davis Texas.* El Paso: The Hill Printing Company, 1963.

_____. *Old Fort Davis.* San Antonio: The Naylor Company, 1947.

_____. *The Story of Fort Davis: Jeff Davis County and the Davis Mountains.* Fort Davis: Marvin Hunter, 1936.

Sparks, Boren. "Emily, the Indian Squaw," <u>Frontier Times</u>. Vol. 17, No. 4, January 1940.

Tyler, Ron, ed. *Handbook of Texas*. Vol. 6. Austin: Texas State Historical Association, 1996.

Welsh, Michael. *A Special Place, A Sacred Trust: Preserving the Fort Davis Story* (An Administrative History). Santa Fe: National Park Service, 1996.

Utley, Robert. *Special Report on Fort Davis, Texas*. Santa Fe: National Park Service, 1960.

How Indian Emily Saved Fort Davis

About the Author

Larry Francell had a forty-year career in the museum profession both as a museum director and consultant. He retired as Director of the Museum of the Big Bend at Sul Ross State University leading the effort to restore and create new exhibits for the original Texas Centennial Building. He served as Jeff Davis County Commissioner, Precinct One for 12 years, was the Jeff Davis County Emergency Management Coordinator and Grants Coordinator and served for three months as Jeff Davis County Judge. He is author of *Fort Lancaster: Texas Frontier Sentinel* and *Fort Davis* an Arcadia Publishing Images of America series. He wrote the Introduction for *Marfa Flights: Aerial Views of Big Bend Country* by Paul Chaplo. He has written numerous articles on the history of the region and lives with his wife Beth in her family home in Fort Davis.

www.ingramcontent.com/pod-product-compliance
Lightning Source LLC
Chambersburg PA
CBHW071255070526
44583CB00017B/2485